CHURCH MUSIC SOCIETY PUBLICATION: 023A
Hon. General Editor: Richard Lyne

for the Choir and Congregation of St. Mary's Church, No...

Saint Mary's Mass

Music by ANTHONY CÆSAR

Kyrie

Andante con moto

Unison Voices

Lord, —— have mer - cy,

Lord, —— have mer - cy, Christ, —— have mer - cy, Christ, —— have mer - cy,

rit. al fine

Lord, —— have mer - cy, Lord, —— have mer - cy, have mer - cy.

Alternative version of Kyrie

Ky - ri - e e - le - i - son,

Ky - ri - e e - le - i - son, Chris - te e - le - i - son, Chris - te e - le - i - son,

rit. al fine

Ky - ri - e e - le - i - son, Ky - ri - e e - le - i - son.

Gloria

For you — a-lone are the Ho - ly One, you a-lone are the Lord,—

cresc.

you a-lone are the Most High, Je - sus Christ, with the Ho - ly Spi - rit,

allargando *ff*

in the glo - ry of God — the Fa - ther. A - men. A - men.

Gospel Responses

mf

Glo - ry to Christ — our Sa - viour.

mf *f*

Praise — to Christ — our Lord. —

Sanctus – Benedictus

Andante solenne *pp*

Ho - ly, Ho - ly, Ho - ly Lord, God — of pow'r and

più mosso *mf* *f*

might, heav'n — and earth are full — of your glo - ry. Ho-san-na in the

mf

high - est. Bless - ed is he who comes — in the name — of the

f *ff*

Lord. Ho-san-na in the high-est, Ho - san - na in the high - est.

Acclamations

Agnus Dei

Acknowledgment

The *Gloria*, the *Sanctus*, the *Benedictus* and the *Agnus Dei* from *The Order for Holy Communion Rite A* from the Alternative Service Book 1980 are © International Consultation on English Texts and are reproduced with permission of the Central Board of Finance of the Church of England.

Origination by Jeanne Fisher, Ludlow, Shropshire
Printed by Halstan & Co. Ltd., Amersham, Bucks

Pack of 10 copies
Not available separately

ISBN 0-19-395363-3